Charleston Recollections and Receipts

1

CHARLESTON
Recollections
and Receipts

Rose P. Ravenel's Cookbook

edited by
Elizabeth Ravenel Harrigan

The University of South Carolina Press

First published by the author, 1983
Cloth edition published by the University of South Carolina Press, 1989
Paperback edition published in Columbia, South Carolina,
by the University of South Carolina Press, 2011

www.sc.edu/uscpress

Manufactured in the United States of America

20 19 18 17 16 15 14 13 12 11   10 9 8 7 6 5 4 3 2 1

Library of Congress Control Number: 89016566

ISBN: 978-0-87249-648-4 (pbk)

CONTENTS

Rusk

Sift a pint & a half of Flour into a bowl, make a hollow in the centre, in which put a table spoonful of butter and five table spoons full of sugar, then pour about a half pint of water moderately warm upon the sugar and butter. Add the yolks of two eggs, beat the whites and put them in, then stir the ingredients which have been placed in the centre for a short time and pour in rather more than a half pint of yeast, three gills will not be too much, when these articles have been well mixed, stir in the flour around the bowl, cover it and set to rise for four or five hours, when well risen, grease a pan, divide the Mass into small portions about the size of a common apple and place them in the pan, set it again to rise and when near the top of the pan have it baked.

Original receipt in Rose P. Ravenel's Cookbook which was given to her by her mama, Christmas 1871.

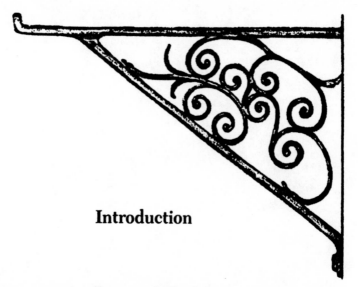

Introduction

This is a unique collection of Charleston memories and receipts. The majority of the receipts were compiled by Rose Pringle Ravenel (1850–1943) and were based on an earlier collection given to her by her mother, Eliza Butler Ravenel, wife of William Ravenel, ante-bellum Charleston planter, merchant and shipowner.

During her long life, Miss Ravenel collected over 200 receipts from Charleston ladies of her acquaintance. The editor, her great-niece, has put together a selection from these and others to create twelve delicious Charleston meals.

Rose P. Ravenel kept notebooks throughout her life and set down stories of the Carolina Lowcountry, plus accounts of the Ravenel family, which has been in South Carolina since the 1680's, as well as reminiscences of her life and the life of her father. The notebooks were edited and published in 1952 as *Piazza Tales: A Charleston Memory* (The Shaftesbury Press). Excerpts from *Piazza Tales* are included in this book in order to shed light on Miss Ravenel's world and to illustrate her humor and insights. Also included are Charleston drawings by Miss Rose Ravenel.

All receipts have been tested. Special thanks are due Mrs. George Bellows and Mrs. David Landon for their fine talent in this area. The transcript is a free one, with an emphasis on the life of a bygone era and the author's highly individual temperament. Receipts calling for large quantities or with archaic instructions have a modern translation.

Elizabeth Ravenel Harrigan

The Career of William Ravenel

W HEN HE WAS sixteen years of age, on the first of May 1823, my father went into the office of Ravenel and Stevens. The office of this importing firm was on Vanderhorst wharf. The business increased so rapidly that he was taken into the firm seven years later. This enterprise flourished until the Confederate War, at which time the firm (then called Ravenel & Company) was totally destroyed. At the time the war broke out, the firm owned two ships and had the controlling interest in five other vessels and a steam tug. These ships maintained regular trade with Europe. Every spring, for several years, a ship loaded with cotton was sent to St. Petersburg in Russia. Thence she went to Sweden for Swedish iron, which she returned to Charleston for sale in South Carolina and Georgia. The first ship built for the firm was the *John Ravenel*, which was burnt in Ashley River in 1865 when the City of Charleston was evacuated by the Confederate authorities. The second ship was given the name of *John Rutledge*, likewise built in Baltimore, Maryland. She was wrecked on an iceberg on a run between Liverpool, England, and New York.

My Father's House

WILLIAM RAVENEL, my father, built No. 7 East Battery. The family moved there from Rutledge Avenue in 1845. Sister Kate was born in Orange Street. The house on Orange Street was my grandfather Pringle's home. My grandfather sold the Orange Street house and bought the house in Cannonsboro. Pringle, Lizzie and Mary were born in the house on Rutledge Avenue. William, Edward, Rose, Julius, Arthur and little Eliza were born in No. 7 East Battery. The house has been given the number of 13 East Battery. Before the Confederate War my father bought the Roper house next door. We now had much land north, south and west of the house. When the house was built we had no carriage way—we had to use the archway. All the stucco work in the drawing room of the house was done by an Irishman. The woodwork was executed by our own Negro carpenters. The columns, destroyed in the earthquake of 1886, were of brick washed over with cement. The capitals of the columns were of composite Corinthian work. The Ravenel house is at the center of the Battery. There is nothing between us and the Canary Islands, save Fort Sumter.

Battery House after Earthquake

Menu

Dinner

Deviled Crab

Grist Cake

Green Salad with Mayonnaise Sauce

Pickled Shrimp (p. 87)

Charlotte Russe

Prepare the Charlotte Russe and green salad the night before. If the grist cake is prepared early, be sure to stir it thoroughly before starting to bake it in a pan of water one and a half hours before dinner.

Deviled crabs are best prepared two hours ahead and popped into a hot oven twenty minutes before serving.

Deviled Crab

1 dozen large crabs—	Butter
(1 to 1½ pounds meat)	Salt, pepper, mace
4 boiled eggs chopped fine	Bread crumbs
2 stalks celery chopped fine	
2 large tablespoons	
mayonnaise	

Boil the crabs twenty minutes. Remove from heat, cool and pick. Be careful to remove "dead man" meat and fat. Use only the white meat and the claw meat.

Lightly add four boiled chopped eggs, chopped celery, a little salt, pepper and mace (to taste) with mayonnaise. Put mixture lightly in crab shells. Lightly cover with crumbs which have been salted. Put a lump of butter on the top of each shell. Put in a large biscuit pan or shallow baking pan. Bake in 350° oven for 15 to 20 minutes or until hot. Do Not burn the tops or let the meat dry out. Put a dab of chutney on top.

Serve immediately.

Makes 8 deviled crabs.

Hominy for Grist Cake

1 C. grits	3 C. water	1 tsp. salt

Today Quaker or any good Quick grits should be used. Into 3 cups of boiling salted water, sprinkle 1 cup grits stirring often to avoid lumps. Cook 20–30 minutes until it's done, but not stiff. Add more water if it gets too thick.

Grist Cake (continued)

2 C. cooked grist, hot	2 eggs
⅔ C. milk	Grated sharp cheese
⅓ stick butter	Salt, pepper to taste

Beat butter and hot grist together. Beat eggs and add to milk. Stir mixture into grist. Salt and pepper to taste. Grate

sharp cheese into all and bake 1½ hours in a baking dish set in a pan of water.

Green Salad

1 envelope gelatin	1 C. cucumbers, diced
1½ C. boiling water	1 C. canned pineapple,
1½ C. pineapple juice	diced
2 Tbs. vinegar	½ C. Mayonnaise
½ tsp. salt	½ Tbs. sugar
¼ tsp. onion juice	juice of 1 lemon

Dissolve gelatin in boiling water, add lemon juice, pineapple juice, vinegar, salt, and onion juice. Chill. When beginning to thicken, fold in cucumbers, pineapple, and mayonnaise.

Put in mold and stand till cold. Serve with mayonnaise sauce on lettuce.

Mayonnaise Sauce

2 egg yolks	1 Tbs. vinegar
1 saltspoon of salt (¼ tsp.)	1 tsp. mustard
½ tsp. pepper	1 pt. olive oil

Beat well together and add, while beating, 1 pt. of olive oil.

Charlotte Russe

1 oz. gelatin	8 beaten egg whites
½ lb. sugar (1 C.)	1 qt. whipping cream
½ C. warm milk	1 lb. pound cake

Mix gelatin and sugar together. Dissolve in warm milk (or water). Beat egg whites. Beat cream until quite stiff (Be sure gelatin mixture is completely cool, or cream will curdle.)

Line a dish with thin slices of cake. Add the beaten egg whites gradually to the cream, and the dissolved gelatin and sugar *stirring* all thoroughly. Pour over the cake. Put in refrigerator until ready for use. (Sherry may be used to flavor the whipped cream.)

Laurium, An Old Family Place

THIS IS what Mamma told Sister Kate: "The earliest memory I have is of Laurium. I was told that I was five years old. I wondered where I had been all the five years that had passed. I had been alive and never remembered a birthday before.

Laurium was an old family place in Prince William's Parish not far from Pocotaligo. This is some fifty miles south of Charleston. It was the residence of my great-grandmother who left it to my mother, she being her favorite grandchild. Mrs. Martha McPherson, my great-grandmother, had one daughter and one son.

My grandparents resided at Laurium, where my grandfather had a race course. He was fond of sporting, owned a number of race horses. He gave large dinner parties to the other sportsmen at the time of the races. And he soon discovered that he had no room large enough to accommodate those to whom he wished to be hospitable. Therefore he built a room the width of the house, which was called the long room. On rainy days, when we were not allowed to go outside, we played in this room. This was a great treat.

Grandma continued to reside at Laurium after the death of my grandfather who was shipwrecked in the *Rose in Bloom*. Then, after my mother's marriage, she bought a place where she had a small neat house built. She named this property Little Canaan. The grounds were laid out in pretty fashion. Many a happy day have I spent there with that dear old lady

who, amid all her sorrows, was most cheerful. Grandma's maiden name was Miles. She married her first cousin John McPherson in 1776 when she was sixteen years of age. She had a fine voice for singing, sweet and powerful. She played the guitar. I have heard say that she would place her guitar on a table at a distance and that when she commenced to sing the tones of her voice would cause the strings of the guitar to vibrate.

On one occasion during the Revolutionary War she went in a chaise to see Grandpa whose company was encamped some miles distant from Laurium. In the course of the journey she met two Continentals who had just tied their horses and were eating their dinner of bread and cheese. They invited her to partake of their meal and handed some bread and cheese to her in the chaise. They requested that she play and sing for them. She took up her guitar and improvised the following—

> I met two men upon the road,
> And how do you think I served them?
> I took away their bread and cheese
> And t'was enough to starve them.

They cried, 'No, we have plenty to spare.' The song was sung to the tune of Yankee Doodle. Grandma then proceeded to the encampment."

Picture of the McPherson Monument
The marble relief was commissioned as a memorial to Gen.
John McPherson, who died in the shipwreck of *The Rose in Bloom.*
The Wreck of the Rose in Bloom, 1809. By John Devaere (Belgian,
1754–1830). Marble. © Image courtesy of the Gibbes Museum of
Art / Carolina Art Association

Menu

Dinner

Oyster Soup

Country Ham with Brandied Peaches (p. 86)

Hoppin' John

Cold Slaw with Sliced Tomatoes

Batter Pudding

The oyster soup can be started an hour before hand with oysters added immediately before dinner and should be served in a large soup tureen at the table.

The country ham must be started the day before your dinner. However, it can be cooked, refrigerated, and lightly wrapped in tin foil several days before hand. The Hoppin' John (which is reputed to bring good luck if eaten on New Year's Day) can also be cooked the day before and reheated (20–30 minutes) before dinner. The cold slaw should be made the night before or several hours before dinner and refrigerated.

Oyster Soup

1 qt. oysters	½ tsp. mace
1 qt. milk	2 Tbs. butter
1 C. cream	Crushed crackers
Dash nutmeg	

Drain oysters saving the liquid.

Add one quart oysters to milk, cream, nutmeg, butter (more if desired richer), mace, and ⅓ cup oyster liquid. Heat just until edges of oysters curl. If they boil, they are too much done. Serve with cracker crumbs sprinkled on top.

Country Ham

Country ham, whole	several peppercorns
1 C. vinegar	several whole cloves
(Spiced Island White	bread crumbs (3 slices)
vinegar)	brown sugar, 1½ cup
2 or 3 onions	

Soak ham in pot of water with 1 C. vinegar. (Be sure ham is completely covered with water.) In the morning, pour off water and vinegar. Fill again with water completely covering the ham, put ham fat side up, and add cut up onions, 1 C. sugar, peppercorns and whole cloves. Simmer 20 min. per pound on top of stove in an uncovered baster pan or until done. (Bone becomes loose.)

Let cool in liquid. Remove all skin and most fat. Lightly score and glaze with ½ C. brown sugar and grated bread crumbs. Bake uncovered in 350° oven for (about) 30 minutes. Cool and serve sliced thin.

To make bread crumbs: brown 3 slices of white or brown bread in slow oven (225°) for 20–25 minutes. Grate and salt to taste.

Hoppin' John

2 C. raw cow peas	¼ lb. jowl or fatback
(dried field peas)	1 small onion, chopped

4 C. water   2 C. raw rice
2 tsp. salt

Soak the peas overnight in 3 C. water. In the morning, add more water and cut up jowl.

Boil peas in salt water and meat about 30 minutes or until *just* tender. Do NOT cook to a mash.

Add the 2 C. of peas, onion, and 2¼ C. of pea liquid with meat to 2 C. of rice. Put in rice steamer or double boiler and cook 1 hour or until rice is done.

Cold Slaw

1 hard head cabbage   Butter size of an egg
Salt and pepper   2 egg yolks
1 C. vinegar   ½ C. cream

Cut a hard head of cabbage in narrow strips and sprinkle salt and pepper over it. Put in a sauce pan a teacup of vinegar, and butter the size of an egg. When the vinegar and butter boil stir in the cream and 2 egg yolks, until it thickens. (You may need to add 3 Tbs. flour to help thicken.) When thick, pour over the shredded cabbage, mixing well. Let it become cold before serving. Garnish with sliced tomatoes.

—John J. Pringle

Batter Pudding

1 pt. buttermilk (or sour cream)
1 tsp. soda
2 eggs
4 large Tbs. sugar
Pinch salt
Fruit (either applesauce, sliced apples, blackberries, cherries, blueberries)
1¼ C. all purpose flour
Cream

16

Mix 1 pint of rich buttermilk or sour cream, 1 tsp. of soda, 2 eggs, 4 large spoons of sugar, and a little salt. Stir in flour until as thick as batter cakes (meaning a soft batter, not a dough). Grease a small baking pan or dish and pour in half of the batter. Spread some fruit over it (either cherries or sliced apples are nice), then add the remainder of the batter. Bake in a moderate oven (350°) for 1 hour. Serve with sugar and cream.

—Mrs. Milliken

Roxana

GENERAL JOHN McPherson, my great grand-father, had a fine race horse by the name of Roxana. The horse became very ill. The general consulted his friends, and all the authorities said the horse was going to die. "General, nothing can be done. You had better shoot Roxana as her suffering will be great and there is no hope of her ever getting well." My great-grandmother heard what the gentlemen said. After the general walked into the house, very sad at the thought of parting with his favorite horse, she said to the Negro who had care of Roxana; "Don't shoot her. I think I can cure her." By patience and perseverance she restored Roxana to perfect health. Mrs. McPherson was fond of horses, and having cured Roxana gave her such a reputation that her husband's friends would ask her opinion before buying a horse.

Roxana was to run a race. The Negro boy who always rode Roxana had been sick with smallpox. General McPherson consented against his will to let the boy ride, as he could not bear to disappoint him. Towards the end of the race the stirrup broke, but the little jockey put it in his mouth and came in triumphant. He won the race. The prize was a large silver bowl with race horses around it—a handsome piece of silver.

Jockey Club Cup

Menu

Dinner

Roast Duckling

Potato Pie in Orange Shells

Asparagus with Celery Sauce

Squash Casserole

Custard Meringue

The hunter and others will enjoy this dinner which is good for any special occasion.

The potato dish can be prepared the day before. The duck is best begun a few hours ahead. (The basting gravy for the duck is so good, it should be saved later for rice.)

Roast Wild Duck

2 wild ducks, or domesticated	1 onion
Salt	2 stalks celery
2 apples	

Soak ducks in salt water 2 or 3 hours. Salt inside and stuff with apples, onions, and celery cut into chunks. Place into covered pan in 1″ water. Cook at 375° for one hour. Remove ducks and throw away all liquid, etc. Return ducks to pan and pour sauce over. Cook one hour longer, basting each ½ hour. Last ½ hour turn ducks and baste backside.

Sauce

¼ C. butter	3 Tbs. currant jelly
4 Tbs. flour	¾ C. orange juice
1½ C. Consomme	8 oz. wine
½ tsp. salt	Dash cayenne

Potato Pie in Orange Shells

1 lb. boiled scraped yellow sweet potatoes, well mashed	½ pt. milk grated peel and juice of 1 lemon
¼ lb. butter	sugar to taste
5 eggs	6 or 8 orange skins

Hollow oranges. Put potato filling in shells and bake at 350° for 20 minutes or until juice begins to come from oranges.

Asparagus

1 lb. asparagus

Wash all vegetables in warm water, then in cold water to make them crisp. The warm water makes the insects leave the vegetables.

Pare the asparagus shoots in the normal way and cut off the hard woody bottoms of the shoots. Then, boil in salted water

until tender. Tie them into a bundle and stand them upright in a deep pot so that stems are boiled and the tips steamed. Cook for 20 minutes on medium heat.

Celery Sauce

Celery	½ pt. cream
1 Tbs. butter	1 tsp. salt
2–3 Tbs. wheat flour	Dash white pepper

Wash carefully, cut in small pieces the white part of three or four stalks of celery. Boil until quite tender. A large tablespoon of butter, two or three of wheat flour, a pint of cream, salt, and white pepper. Mix very smoothly and boil stirring all the time. When done, pour it over the boiled celery and let it simmer for a few minutes.

Creamy Squash Casserole

1½ lb. yellow squash, sliced
¾ cup grated sharp cheddar cheese
1 C. sour cream
4 oz. pimentos, drained and sliced
8½ oz. raw, scraped Jerusalem artichokes (or water chestnuts), sliced
1 medium onion, finely chopped
1 stick butter
4 oz. of buttered salted bread crumbs

Cook the squash in salt water until tender and drain well. Mix squash, cheese, sour cream, pimientos, water chestnuts, and onions, stirring gently.

Place in 2 quart baking dish and dot with butter. Sprinkle bread crumbs on top. Bake at 350° for 30 minutes. Serves 8.

Custard Meringue

6 egg yolks, beaten	6 egg whites, beaten
½ C. sugar	½ C. sugar
2 Tbs. cornstarch	1 tsp. vanilla
1 qt. milk	

Beat together the yolks of 6 eggs, add ½ C. sugar, 2 Tbs. cornstarch. Scald 1 qt. of milk and stir above into it. Let it boil 20 minutes.

Beat the whites to a stiff froth, add ½ C. sugar, flavor, and pour the whites of the eggs over the top of the pudding after you have arranged it in a dish for the table. Put in a 350° oven and color to a light brown. To be eaten cold.

—From Mrs. Ducin 1871

Buying The Farm

BEFORE THE war my father took great interest in planting. The Marsh plantation on the North Santee River, above Charleston, belonged to my mother. He had an overseer but he went, nevertheless, once a year to the plantation, a rice plantation.

Some years prior to the war he bought a farm in St. Andrew's Parish. There was a small house on the property, which we occupied a few months of each year until a large house was built. The big house, the present building, was constructed by his Negro workmen. The family moved into the house in 1854.

My mother took great interest in having trees planted. When she left it in 1865, at the time of the evacuation of Charleston, it was a beautiful place—the extensive lawns were bordered with rose bushes. I have heard friends who visited at Farmfield say that it ought to have been named Rosefield or Roseland.

Farmfield Farm was self-supporting, The family was supplied with every kind of vegetable. I have never forgotten the large dishes of figs, plums, watermellon, and muskmelon that were products of the farm when I was a child.

My father had a Negro foreman named Charles who was devoted to him. It was but five miles from our town house to our country house, and my father would visit Farmfield two or three times a week. He always carried a nice dinner to Charles, and often took ginger cakes for the Negro children.

Farmfield

Menu

Dinner

Shrimp Bisque

Roast Turkey with Bread Sauce or Gravy

Wild Rice

Fresh Green Beans

Artichoke Pickle (p. 86)

Cream Chocolates (p. 88)

A grand, festive dinner. Hunt for tiny creek shrimp.
Two sauces are offered with the turkey. The bread sauce is
seldom seen (but so good) and the turkey gravy is too good to
discard. A hash receipt follows for the left-over turkey.
The artichoke pickle needs to be prepared ahead.

Shrimp Bisque

1 pt. milk
1 Tbs. flour
1 Tbs. French mustard

Salt and pepper
1 plate of shrimp (1 lb.)

Boil shrimp in salted water. Remove when pink. Put in collander and run under cold water to keep them crisp. Peel and devein.

Put milk, pepper, salt, and mustard on fire. Let it come to a boil, then thicken slightly with flour dissolved in water. Dice or break shrimp into small pieces and add to milk mixture. Warm and serve each cup with sherry.

Turkey

Use pop-up thermometer turkey.

Dressing: Saute onion in butter. Toast and cut in small pieces 5 slices bread. Add to onion. Add a little milk (¼ C.), salt, pepper. Make it light. Chop 3 hard-boiled eggs, mix in lightly with fork. Add pinch of sage and thyme. Stuff turkey and roast in covered, shallow pan. Don't mash dressing in turkey. Serve with wild rice.

Bread Sauce

1 thick slice bread
  (about 3-4 slices)
1 pt. water
1 white onion

salt
Dash white pepper
4 oz. cream
1 Tbs. butter

Mash up slices of bread in a pint of water with a white onion, salt, white pepper. When the onion is quite soft, pour the whole through a seive, pressing the bread through. Put this in a saucepan. Add a gill of fresh cream, a large spoonful of fresh butter. Simmer over the fire stirring carefully. If you have no cream use milk, no water. Serve in a sauce tureen to be eaten with roasted turkey or fowl.

—Mrs. Edward J. Pringle
of Beneventrun

Gravy

The brown crust that sticks to the sides of the pan is the foundation of all good gravies. This is the meat essence itself. Tilt the dripping pan slightly so as to let the grease run off into a bowl. then scratch down all that you can get of the brown crust with the remaining gravy. Stir it, add hot water to dissolve, but get it all. Then you have the rich colored gravy that has a taste to it. The sick-looking gravies that are served at some tables show that the most valuable part has been thrown away. Thicken with a little flour disolved in water. Add milk, salt and pepper. Simmer.

Wild Rice

Try to find R. M. Quigg's Wild Rice. Bring 2¼ C. water to a boil. Add ⅔ C. wild rice and ½ tsp. salt. Cover tightly and cook over low heat approximately 50 minutes. Keep lid on while cooking, as steam aids in the cooking process. For a firmer, nutty texture, cook 45–50 minutes or for softer, more tender rice, cook 60–65 minutes. Serves three.

Fresh Green Beans

1 lb. green beans
4 tablespoons butter
1 small onion, sliced thin
1 clove garlic

½ cup parsley, chopped fine
Optional: 1 tablespoon toasted sesame seeds

Cut beans on slant in approximately 1 inch pieces. Place in vegetable steamer with 1 cup water. Cook 10 to 15 minutes or until tender.

Melt butter in skillet, add onions and stir constantly for 1

minute. Crush garlic and add to onion. Add beans and stir lightly until coated with the butter. Remove garlic.

Add parsley and sesame seeds and toss lightly. Serve at once.

For a Hash

Meat (cooked turkey)	Clove
Flour	Meat stock
Pepper	Bacon or ham
Salt	Browning
Onion	Butter

Cut the meat very thin, take away all of the fat. Flour the meat on both sides. Shake the pepper lightly over, salt. Cut an onion in four pieces and stick a clove in each piece. Put in the bottom of a pie dish. Then, put in the meat. Add several spoonsful of stock, a few slices of bacon or ham. Cover with a flat dish and bake. Cook for 2 hours.

If there is no gravy or stock, mix a tablespoon of flour with the yolk of an egg, a scrap of butter or bacon fat into a batter. Pour hot water over it, a few drops of browning. Pour over and bake.

Sauces for Hashes

2 oz. vinegar	1 onion cut up fine
4 chopped anchovies	1 doz. peppercorns
a little mace	Bunch savory herbs
a bay leaf	1 tsp. horseradish
½ tsp. cloves	½ pt. Claret

Put all ingredients in a saucepan and let them simmer for ten minutes, or until anchovies are dissolved. Then add 1/2 pint claret and let simmer for 10 more minutes.

Then strain and use or bottle for use.

The Death of Young William

MY BROTHER William Ravenel, Jr., aged seventeen, was brought home to East Battery. He was desperately ill with typhoid fever. He had been doing guard duty. The night of August 24, 1863 the Yankees shelled Charleston. One of the shells fell in the water in front of our house, and the family was urged to leave East Battery. My father objected but, in time, yielded. At four o'clock in the morning an ambulance was brought around to the house. Mamma and Sister Kate sat on the floor of the ambulance. Bill lay on a mattress. His head rested on Sister Kate's lap. They wended their way uptown with the dying boy. After travelling a mile and a half, Mr. George Trenholm, who lived in the house my grandfather had owned on Rutledge Avenue, took them in and gave them shelter. Bill died in what used to be grandmother Pringle's bedroom.

The Shelling of the City

IN THE winter of 1864, Pringle, our brother, came home on a short furlough. One morning we walked downtown to our house on East Battery. We walked down King and Meeting Streets, stopping again and again to listen for the shells that were coming. We gathered that they were falling in the eastern part of the city. I remember that there were earth works in Meeting Street from Lightwood Alley to the Battery. There was a high battery in White Point Garden. Our house, we observed, was extensively damaged by shells. We entered

the house and sat on the piazza on the second floor. We looked
out over the harbor—it was a lovely winter day and the water
appeared so peaceful and calm. The shells were coming in
towards the west. On our way back uptown we found the
streets grown up in grass and weeds. There were very few
people about. Everywhere we saw the work of shells that had
been hurled into the city.

Battery House before Earthquake

Menu

Dinner

Fricassee Chicken with Rice

Tomatoes Baked

Iced Apples

Men especially enjoy this chicken. Everyone will be delighted with this unusual dessert.

White Fricassee

2 chickens	¼ lb. butter
(or thighs or legs)	1 Tbs. wheat flour
3 C. milk	¼ tsp. mace
1 C. water	¼ tsp. nutmeg
½ pt. cream	4 hard-boiled
	eggs—mashed

Two chickens remove the skin and lay in warm water to draw out the blood. Wipe with a dry towel. Place in a stew pan with milk and water warming the chickens entirely and stew them until *quite tender*. Put in another stew pan ½ pint cream, ¼ pound butter, stir until blended. Add a little wheat flour, mace, and grated nutmeg. Boil for a few moments, then add mashed eggs. Pour over chickens and simmer over the fire and serve. The eggs are a great addition.

—copied from Mrs. W. B. Pringle

Steamed Rice

2 C. uncooked long grain rice
2 C. water
½ tsp. salt

Put 2 C. rice in 2 C. salted water in top of rice steamer. Steam 45 minutes to one hour. When done, fluff with fork.

Tomatoes Baked

2 onions, chopped
12 tomatoes, washed, cored and cut in small pieces
1½ C. bread crumbs (6 slices of bread)
2 Tbs. butter
2 beaten eggs
1 tsp. sugar
1 tsp. salt
pepper to taste

Mix together, put in greased casserole and bake for 1½ hours at 350 degrees.

Iced Apples

1 doz. apples
Currant jelly
Milk, cream or custard

One dozen fine, firm apples. Pared and cored leaving a hole. Stew in water enough to cover them until you can pierce them with a straw. Set to cool, then fill center with currant or other jelly. Make an icing and ice like a cake. Eat with milk, cream, or custard.

Icing

⅛ lb. melted butter
¼ lb. Confectioner's 10X powdered sugar (or more)
Juice of 1 lemon
a little cold water

Combine ¼ lb. powdered sugar, butter and a little cold water. Beat well. Add lemon juice and stir it all one way until smooth. Lay on apple with a broad knife or wooden paddle.

Farmfield

I WAS WITH my father and mother at Farmfield in St. Andrew's Parish the months of January, February, and March of 1865. I was taught to card cotton and wool, to spin it into yarn, and made to knit one or two pairs of socks for the soldiers every month. Every day I read aloud in French to Mamma, and was made to knit while I read. Mamma said that if I knew how to knit without looking at the knitting it would help me if I was ever old and blind.

I helped to make envelopes and made all kinds of paper. When a letter was received, the envelope was turned if it was possible to do so. Often the envelopes were made of wallpaper.

I loved to watch the Negro women make myrtleberry candles. I gathered the berries for them very often. I took pleasure also in picking rushes, pealing them, dipping them in lard, and drying them. They were used to light candles and the lard lamps, for matches were difficult to obtain. In fact, I do not remember seeing matches during those days. Lightwood made too much smoke—hence rushes were used. The rushes grew in swampy places and in brackish water. Always there was a fire in the kitchen, and we got a light from that fire for the rushes.

Salt was made at Farmfield. It was taken from Wappoo Creek in buckets, emptied into large iron pots and boiled down. The creek was near at high tide and it was easy to bring

the water up in buckets. The iron pots used in the boiling process were kept near the stable.

When Mamma wanted hair pins a Negro boy was sent down the avenue to climb a tree and gather locust thorns. On these thorns were stamped seals—seals fashioned of wax in many colors. The thorns were thought to be very pretty in one's hair.

Pokeberries were gathered in order to make ink. Rose geranium leaves were distilled for the sick.

The books we read that winter at Farmfield (the ones I remember) were Pope's Homer and Sir Walter Scott. We read more French than English—English was a novelty.

Molasses candy was a great treat. Rice in the hull was put on a shuffle. The rice expanded and popped. These pretty white things were dropped in the candy. At long intervals we were given gingerbread. It was not made with real ginger but with red pepper. We thought this gingerbread delicious.

In the Up country raspberry leaves were gathered. They were dried and used for tea. In the Low country strawberry leaves were used.

Molasses Candy

| 1 qt. molasses | 2 Tbs. of essence lemon |
| ¼ lb. brown sugar | ½ lb. butter |

Let the molasses boil, add sugar and when half done put in butter. Boil one hour, stirring. Add the lemon when you take it from the fire. Pour into buttered plates. When *slightly* cooled pick up small amounts and pull until white.

Flower Dolls

EARLY IN the war my dolls were lost. I do not remember in what manner it happened. Miss Maria Middleton made some paper dolls for Lizzie, Alfred Ravenel, and me. We found that flower dolls were easy to obtain. My French nurse put arms and legs made of grass or straw on the flower dolls. They were frail, not easy to handle. We amused ourselves by telling their histories. The dolls had many adventures. Often I would bring a large family of snowdrops to visit Lizzie's periwinkles. The dolls had wide or narrow skirts as each variety of flower came in season. When there was no wind we played with the dolls on the steps of the big house at Farmfield.

Wartime Glassware

I HAVE OFTEN seen Mamma make tumblers. She took a string dipped in oil, tied it around a bottle, and set the string on fire. The bottle would break along the line where the string had been tied. Sandpaper was used to smooth the edge of the tumblers. We never used them on the dinner table. They were used in the pantry. The bottles were pretty, dark and light blue, green, red, and amber. In those days the lady of the house had to be clever and find substitutes for

whatever was needed, as household supplies could not be purchased at any price. For instance, sandpaper was made of glue or paste on thick paper. Sand from the beaches was sprinkled on the paper. I have seen it done, though I have never done it myself The gum from peach and plum trees made a very satisfactory glue.

W. G. Young's cup.

This Silver cup is called a plantation
cup; as most of the things used on the
rice plantation are represented
on it; rice stacks, barn house, rake,
scythe, bee hives, Winnors house, & ...
Dwelling house; rice stacks alternate
between each, representations
It was a favorite gift of God fathers

Plantation Cup

Menu

Dinner

Deviled Chicken

Red Rice

Carrots

Braised Lettuce

Thick Ginger Cake with Wine Sauce

This is a colorful dinner and especially nice in the winter. The wine sauce is so easy, but once tasted never forgotten.

Deviled Chicken

1 chicken
2 tsp. dry mustard
½ tsp. paprika
1 tsp. salt

dash red pepper
2 tsp. vinegar
¼ C. Wesson Oil

Put chicken in baking dish. Pour Wesson Oil over the chicken. Make paste of other ingredients and spread with back of spoon over chicken. Sprinkle with bread crumbs, dot with butter. Bake in covered casserole at 350 degrees about 1 hour 15 minutes.

—Bidi Watt

Red Rice

6 slices bacon
2 medium onions, chopped
1 6 oz. can tomato paste

2 C. raw rice
salt, pepper to taste

Fry bacon in large frying pan. Remove bacon and sauté chopped onions in 2 Tbs. bacon drippings until they are clear. Add tomato paste and two cups of water. Salt and pepper to taste. Simmer for 5 minutes.

Pour 2¼ cups of tomato mixture in top of rice steamer with 2 C. uncooked rice. Mix together. Steam about one hour. Serve in dish with bacon crumbled on top.

Carrots

1 lb. small carrots   ½ tsp. salt   butter

Pare the carrots. Do not cut or scrape and boil whole in boiling water with a ½ tsp. salt and a small lump butter to make them tender and retain colour.

Braised Lettuce

Large head bib or Boston lettuce, or two medium heads
6 slices bacon, simmered in 1 qt. water for 10 min.
1½ C. chicken stock (canned may be used)

Put a large head of lettuce (or two medium size) in boiling water for 5 minutes (salt water). Plunge in cold water and drain. Put simmered bacon in bottom of casserole. Put lettuce on top, cover with stock and bake 1½ hours to 2 hours in slow oven. When cooked almost to a jelly, flavor with salt and pepper and serve.

Thick Ginger Cake

5 C. flour (all-purpose)	1 Tbs. Allspice
12 oz. Molasses	½ tsp. nutmeg
2 Tbs. butter	½ C. citron (if available)
3 Tbs. brown sugar	1 C. white raisins
3 eggs (beaten)	4 oz. milk or cream
1 Tbs. grated orange peel	1 tsp. soda

Rub (cream) the butter and sugar together, put in the eggs well-beaten, then the molasses, seasonings, flour, raisins, citron and last the soda dissolved in milk or cream. Mix all well and bake at 325 degrees for about 50 minutes. Bake in two loaf pans. Serve with whipped cream or "Wine Sauce"

—Miss E. P. Huger

Wine Sauce

1 C. fine sugar	6 Tbs. Sherry
3 Tsp. butter	Nutmeg

Beat the butter and sugar till light, put the mixture in double boiler and stir until it is creamy, then add sherry. Make sure it is not too thick. Serve warm.

The Winter of 1865

I SPENT THE winter of 1865 with my father and mother at Farmfield. Papa went to Charleston early every morning. Mamma would give the orders about dinner to Maum Daphne, then sit down by the dining room fire and hear me recite my French lessons. During the lessons Maum Sophy would come in to report if any of the Negroes were sick, to explain what was needed, and to ask advice. These confidential conversations lasted a long time. After Maum Sophy left and the French lessons were completed, Mamma and I would take a nice relish to old Charles, our Negro foreman, who was very sick. Old Charles was interesting and most clever. Generally we found him reading, with a large Bible on his knees. Sometimes we gave him the newspapers. Usually he said he did not care for them, said "Mausser will give me the news when he comes home." Charles frequently talked of old times. The war was a great trouble to him.

Later in the day Mamma and I would take a drive. We had an old mule that never went out of a walk. Mamma knew nothing about driving. We went until we came to camp, and then asked a soldier to turn the mule and buggy so that we could head for home. During these drives Mamma told me stories of the Revolutionary War that she had heard from her grandmother. She told me about France and sometimes recited poetry. We were so happy, and I never tired of hearing of the past.

At dusk Mamma put a large piece of lightwood on the fire in

the dining room, sat on the hearth rug and read to me in French. We lit the lamp when we heard Papa arrive. We always had soldiers to supper and to spend the night. The young soldiers were delightful, so gay and hopeful. They had no end of funny stories. Often we had old soldiers. They were very grave and courageous. Their conversation, though painful and depressing, was thrilling. I could not help listening when battles were discussed. My parents were enthusiastic over our brave men, and spoke with tenderness and affection of friends who had been killed in battle, sorrowful over the death of some young soldier who had died—"so and so's only son—young and promising." Those old soldiers would shake their heads and ask, "How will the war end?" My own dear Papa would look serious; a gloomy, suffering expression would pass over his handsome face. Often I would leave the room and sit on the stairs and weep. I was frightened and spent many nights wondering how anyone lived to a good old age. Life was so stormy and painful.

One evening Papa told us Mr. and Mrs. B— were to run the blockade that very night. The next morning I said, "The B's have run the blockade successfully." "What do you know about it child? How can you possibly know?" I said, "I listened all night and did not hear any extra bombarding." From my bed at night I could observe the shells falling on James Island. I never minded hearing the heavy guns from the forts or gunboats as much as the guns of the infantry. My blood seemed to curdle when I heard the infantry guns on the Island. The following day I heard there had been a skirmish with the enemy. I was moved into another room—I could hear the gunfire, missed the diversion of watching the shells.

One morning my parents left the farm at eight o'clock. They went to see Cousin Dan Ravenel who was ill. I was the only white person on the plantation. As I felt bad, I stayed in bed. Soon after Papa and Mamma left I heard loud knocks at the back door which was near my own room. Maum Betsy came to me, said, "Miss Rose, ever so many soldiers have come and they want something to eat. They say they are so hungry. They look starved." I gave Maum Betsy the keys and told her to feed breakfast to the soldiers. Negroes are so kind-hearted,

and like nothing better than to feed people. I knew that the soldiers were in good hands.

After breakfast had been given the soldiers, Maum Betsy and two or three Negro women rushed to my room. They were very much excited. They said, "Miss Rose, the soldiers say a terrible battle is going on near here." All that morning the Negro women kept coming in and going out of my room, telling me the news. The rumors of the battle became wilder and wilder. One woman asked "Miss Rose, do you tink Mass Pringle, Mass Edward and Mass James in dat battle?" At about four o'clock in the afternoon my parents arrived at the farm. They found me sick. The next day they sent for Dr. Henry de Saussure. He said I must be brought to Charleston because his son, Alexander, was ill of typhoid and he was unable to leave the city again. However, Papa and Mamma learned that Charleston was to be evacuated in two days.

I do not remember whether it was the seventeenth or eighteenth of March that Mamma and I left the farm. We walked through the dining room (I was in somewhat better health) and breakfast was on the table. It had not been touched. Papa and Mamma were too worried and tired to eat anything. I had had breakfast in my room. Mamma looked around the dining room and said, "Rose, we cannot take anything with us but our clothes and a few pieces of silver." She quickly put the silver in a satchel she was carrying. Therefore we left our comfortable and pretty home furnished not only with our own things but many belongings sent in from other plantations. One room was filled with books. The books were in heaps on the floor of the room, spilling out of the bookcases. When we came down the steps there was a crowd of Negroes to say goodbye—men, women, and children. The Negroes looked sad, were so troubled and unhappy. But they were very quiet. The men were clad in Welsh plains, the women in dark homespun. Maum Daphne and the house servants shook hands with us, the men took off their hats, the women made a low curtsy. With great feeling they said, "God bless you my Missus. God bless you little Miss." We hated to leave them with heavy hearts and tears in their eyes. We said good bye, gave them our blessing and departed. The day

before I heard Papa say "Thank God I am able to leave them well clad and with plenty of food." In those days it was not easy to get clothes and our poor soldiers were half starved.

We drove to town, crossing the Ashley River bridge. The ship, *John Ravenel*, was at anchor in the river and we took a last look at it. A few hours later it was set afire by our forces, as was the bridge. Driving through the streets of Charleston we met heavy carts laden with furniture—people were moving in from the country. When we arrived at the Northeastern Railroad, Papa and Mamma went to see if it were possible for us to carry our small trunks on the journey. I was put in a railroad car, was too sick to notice my surroundings. I heard someone say, "A child is here! Child, what are you doing here? Good God! It is Rose!" I recognized Uncle Alfred's voice. He took me to another car and put me in the conductor's room. The car I had been in was a car filled with sick soldiers. There were mattresses on the floor. Men were lying on them and some of them were groaning.

Mamma and another lady and old Dr. Holbrook soon joined me. After being in the car a short time we heard a cry, "fire." Smoke poured in the windows, and we were obliged to leave. Everything seemed enveloped in flames. The smoke was suffocating. Nevertheless we were told to return to the car, which we did; the smoke was so powerful that we found it difficult to breathe. Some time later our car was detached from the burning cars and we saw a pile of cotton burning. We started and then stopped again after a journey of five miles. The train stopped at regular five mile intervals. The conductor told us on one of these stops that we would most certainly meet the Yankees. Once we did hear a few rifle shots. The panic was great. Dr. Holbrook was not ruffled or disturbed. He was quiet and calm, took some bread and hogshead cheese from a basket and offered a portion to us. We were not hungry and rather afraid of hogshead, hence refused his offer. Dr. Holbrook said, "Bad taste, all nonsense to refuse. The cheese cannot hurt you." The old doctor ate his cheese with relish and put up the rest of it for his supper. He took out of his basket a yellow paperback French novel, read until dark, ate his supper of hogshead cheese and bread, talked a little and

said good night. He slept soundly but was frequently roused by the conductor. At first he bore these visits with patience but they were so frequent that he lost patience and used strong language. He said, "I wish to sleep. Why does that fellow call so often? Damn it, if we were to meet the Yankees a little sleep would help us! Damn if I don't wish that fellow would leave us alone! I don't care about the G__ D__ Yankees."

We arived at Society Hill the following afternoon. The old doctor went to Cheraw. We left him with his novel in his hand. I was sorry to see him depart, for I found his grumbling and remarks amusing. There were no vehicles when we arrived at the depot. Fortunately, Uncle William Bull Pringle happened to pass in his buggy and took us to Aunt Rosa M. Pringle's. I was so very tired as a consequence of sitting up all night on uncomfortable seats in the cars. I heard Aunt Hess Pringle say, "Eliza has brought that poor child here to die. She will not live long."

Winnowing

Menu

Dinner

Mrs. Boykin's Shrimp and Rice

Apples and Carrots

Spinach

Tomato Pickle (p. 86)

Sparkling Jelly

A colorful Fall dinner. Be sure to cook your small shrimp in this way: Boil two cups of salted water in a saucepan. Add shrimp to water and let come to a boil again. Remove shrimp when pink or they will be tough. Pour immediately into a collander. Cool and then peel. (devein if desired)

Mrs. Boykin's Shrimp and Rice

3 lb. shrimp
10 slices bacon
4 eggs
2 sticks butter

2 C. uncooked, long-
  grain rice
2 C. water
½ tsp. salt

Rice
Put 2 C. rice in 2 C. salted water in top of rice steamer. Steam for 45–1 hr. When done, separate with fork to make fluffy.

Shrimp
Hard boil 4 eggs. Melt 2 sticks butter and add small cooked shrimp (cut shrimp in pieces if large). Pour over cooked rice while still in steamer and add ½ of hard-boiled eggs thinly sliced. Compose platter: put down bed of rice with shrimp (warmed in butter), surround with remaining slices of hard-boiled eggs. Put cooked bacon strips in sunburst pattern on top of shrimp.

Apples and Carrots

6 cooking apples
10 large carrots
1/2 tsp. salt
cinnamon

1 stick of butter
3 C. water
½ cup of sugar

Scrape and slice carrots, cook in 3 C. salted water until tender (about 20 min. on medium heat), drain. Meanwhile, peel, core, and slice apples. As soon as carrots are tender, alternate layer of carrots with layer of apples in 1 qt. casserole. Dot with butter, sprinkle with sugar, and a little cinnamon. Bake at 350° for 40 minutes until bubbly.

Spinach

Fresh spinach
1½ Tbs. butter

dash salt
2 eggs

Put fresh washed and deveined spinach in colander over boiling water. Cover and cook until wilted. Then remove colander and let spinach drain. Chop fine. Then put a little butter into saucepan and a very little salt. When melted, put in the spinach and let simmer until thoughly warmed. Serve with quartered hard-boiled eggs.

Sparkling Jelly

2 envelopes gelatin	2 C. sugar
¼ pt. hot water (½ C.)	3 egg whites
¾ pt. boiling water (1½ C.)	⅓ C. sherry
juice 1 lemon	nutmeg

Sprinkle gelatin in ¼ pint hot water and soak for 5 to 10 minutes. Pour ¾ pint boiling water, lemon juice, and sugar on it. Cool. Add sherry to gelatin mixture before mixing with egg whites. Beat egg whites with pinch of salt 5 minutes until stiff and mix thoroughly with cooled jelly. Put into glass dishes and chill in refrigerator until firm. Before serving, sprinkle nutmeg lightly on top.

This is especially nice when served in something glass so you can see the layers. It is very sweet, so a little goes a long way.

Maum Daphne's Experience

I ASKED MAUM Daphne what she did after we left Farmfield
in 1865. She said, "A few days after you and old Miss gone,
the Yankees come in rowboats. I saw the Yankees talking to
some of the niggers. One of the Yankees spoke to me, said,
"Tell me where the silver is buried or hidden! We have been
told you know all about it." Maum Daphne said, "No silver is
buried on this place that I know." The soldier pointed his gun
at her and said, "I will shoot you." He walked off, saying "Old
woman, I will come back and will see that you tell me." Maum
Daphne walked away very frightened. She met an officer and
told him that she didn't know where any silver was concealed.
He told her that he believed she was telling the truth and
advised her to leave immediately, said that she ought to take
the first boat that passed and not to return to her house. If she
did return, he said, she would have a hard time as all the
Negroes thought she knew where the silver was buried. She
hailed the first boat she saw. It was crowded with Negroes and
with many baskets and bundles. They were overladen and
didn't want to take her along with them but consented at last.
Maum Daphne told me that she didn't believe they would get
to Charleston. Upon her arrival she had no money and nothing in the world but the clothes on her back. She was a good
cook, however, and soon found a job. All her belongings were
stolen when she left the farm. Often she saw things in a Negro
house in Charleston that were her belongings. The Negroes
never returned anything to her. The Negroes on the farm had

a hard time, especially the old and the sick. Many of the
Negroes died. Old Charles was the first to die. When we
returned to Charleston in October of 1865 some of the old
Negroes came to us and were taken care of by Papa and
Mamma until they died.

Woman Selling Oysters

Menu

Light Lunch or Supper

Okra Soup

Shrimp Pie

Avocado-Grapefruit Salad with Vinegar and Oil

Citron Pie

Citron may be hard to find except at Thanksgiving and Christmas. If so, a good tart preserve may be used.

Small creek shrimp or medium size shrimp should be used in the shrimp pie.

Okra Soup

1 lb. Stew meat
2 cans peeled tomatoes (cut)
2 packages frozen okra
1 stalk celery, chopped
½ tsp. pepper

6 C. water
1 bay leaf
1 onion (cut in sixths)
1½ tsp. salt

Cover stew meat with 6 cups of water and cook about 1 hour. If not tender, cook longer. (Add more water if necessary.) Add cut tomatoes, okra, celery, bay leaf, onion, and salt and pepper to taste. Reduce to simmer. Add 2 tsp. sugar to cut acidity. Simmer until all vegetables are tender and consistency is soup-like.

Shrimp Pie

As soon as bought, put shrimp in a pot of boiling water, just enough to cover them. Boil not more than 5 minutes. Put in a collander and pump cold water on them. That makes them crisp. Keep in a cool place, shell, and devein.

2 lb. shrimp
1 pt. (2 C.) rice or 2 C. bread crumbs
½ stick butter
Salt, pepper, dry mustard to taste
Enough catsup to make it pink
½ C. milk
1 egg

Boil shrimp. Cook 2 C. rice (or use bread crumbs). Butter rice or crumbs well. Season the shrimp with salt, pepper, mustard, and catsup to one's taste. Mix with rice (or crumbs) and place in pie plate or shallow dish. Bake in 350° oven for one hour or until solid. (Use bread crumbs instead of rice. A little milk and egg is an improvement.)

Avocado-Grapefruit Salad

If possible, use fresh, pink grapefruit. Cut around and loosen sections of halved grapefruit, remove sections from shell. Slice avocado halves, arrange on plate on top of lettuce with grapefruit sections. Cover with French dressing.

Salad Dressing

1 raw egg yolk	1 tsp. mixed mustard
Pinch salt	4 oz. milk
1 Tbs. oil	2 tsp. vinegar

Mix egg yolk and oil slowly and thoroughly. Add salt, mustard, and milk. Then add vinegar. Simmer this on the fire after it is well mixeu until it thickens. This makes a small quantity.

Cake Pie or Citron Pie

10 egg yolks
1 lb. sugar (2 C.)
Essence of lemon
Citron or preserved fruit
   (1 lb. jar Dundee's Three Fruit Marmalade)

Rub (cream) together egg yolks and white sugar until a high brown color. (Most important or eggs will separate from fruit while baking.) Flavor with 1 tsp. essence of lemon. Lay the citron or spread preserves in pie plate. Cover with eggs and sugar mixture. Bake slowly, about 1 hour, in a slow oven, 325 degrees.

A Lesson From the Butler

WE SPENT several months in Columbia after the close of the Confederate War. The struggle for life was very great at that time, yet one never heard a murmur of protest. Everyone tried to pass the time cheerfully. We, the William Ravenels, lived principally on cowpeas and bacon. I have heard Mamma say that when the bacon was put before her at the dinner table that it was trouble to cut it because it was so small.

After finishing our cowpeas, a long time would elapse before Horlsey, our Negro butler, brought the bacon into the room. We became so tired of waiting, wondered why he did not bring in the bacon promptly.

In the evening when I came home from my stroll I would go in the kitchen and talk with the old Negro maumers and with Horlsey. Those family Negroes were very aristocratic. They made me walk in the correct way. I must be good, they said, and speak correctly. In the summertime we sat in the yard and by the kitchen fire in the winter months. Those old Negroes were devoted to me, told me stories of old times on the plantations—lovely tales that never came to an end.

One evening I said "Horlsey, why do you wait so long before bringing in the bacon after you take off the soup?" Horlsey looked grave, said, "Miss Rose, I am educating you." "Educating me, Horlsey? How?" "Miss Rose, the times are hard. You ought to know how we lived before the war—how things ought to be." Horlsey described a very elaborate din-

ner with many courses—soup, fish, and game, and so on. He enjoyed instructing me and said, "You must try and think you are eating all those things I mentioned while you are waiting for the bacon." I told Mamma. Thereafter we waited patiently and never found fault at the long interval between cowpeas soup and bacon.

Horlsey took great pride in his work. Oftentimes he called me to see how nice the dinner table looked. "Look how bright I have made the silver," he would say. "And such a beautiful table cloth. No dinner to serve. Too bad everything is changed. I try my best to educate you, Miss Rose. No one seems to know it." Horlsey shook his head, said "Times are bad."

Shopkeepers and War Records

FEELING WAS very high between north and south after the Confederate War. Whenever I went to shop in Kings Street, I asked Mamma if I could do anything for her. She would say "Rose, you are to remember that you must shop only in those stores where the war records are good." Mr. B. Schuckerman kept a worsted store. His war record was fine. He was a German and sympathetic with Germany. When the Germans in Charleston had a parade in 1870, rejoicing at the victory over the French, Mr. Schuckerman was asked to decorate his store with German flags. He said he was sorry to be disobliging but that he could not do it. He said he knew how it felt to be conquered—all the suffering and pain caused by war and defeat—which many were suffering at that time.

Mr. A. W. Jager was a splendid Confederate. How I hated to go to that store! He never had anything I wished. One day I bought some white ribbon to trim a party dress. It was rotten. The silk thread I purchased was worse. I felt like crying (am afraid I did cry). I was sure that Mr. Jager must have bought it before the war. When I told my mother that the ribbon and thread were rotten, she said, "It is impossible. His war record is too good for it to be rotten." She said I must have sat in an east wind—that was proverbial for rotting silk thread. I was only too glad when the old gentlemen and their war records died and vanished. Now I can go to any shop. There are no war records to consider.

Col. Bull's Calling Card

JUST BEFORE the evacuation of Charleston, W. I. Bull set fire to his house on Ashley Hall plantation, saying he would rather burn his house than leave it to the Yankees to burn. After the Confederate War he lived in a small house on the plantation.

One year—I think 1869—a French vessel of war came to Charleston. We saw a good deal of the officers, and I remember playing croquet with them on several occasions at the Battery. I danced with them at parties and balls.

The French officers went everywhere in their rowboats. One morning they went to Ashley Hall, got out of their boats, and walked around the grounds. They met a Negro man, asked him if Colonel Bull were at home. The Negro gave their cards to Colonel Bull. He had no card but picked up a wooden shingle and wrote on it: "Colonel William Izard Bull, Ashley Hall, St. Andrew's Parish, South Carolina." This was written in black paint. He sent this card to the French officers and asked them to come up to the house. The colonel met them very cordially. The French officers said they enjoyed their visit to Ashley Hall and appreciated Colonel Bull's hospitality and enjoyed his interesting conversation.

The church of St Andrew's Parish

St Andrew's church

St. Andrew's Church

Nathaniel Heyward Gateway

Menu

Light Lunch or Supper

Tomato Soup

Eggs A La Bennett

Pears Poached in Wine

Groundnut Cakes (p. 88)

This is an excellent lunch on a hot, summer afternoon. If you enjoy color, this lunch will be a delight to prepare and present.

Tomato Soup

1 qt. canned tomatoes	6 or 8 crackers (crushed)
1½ qt. water	¼ stick butter
pinch soda	¼ tsp. pepper
½ tsp. basil	1 tsp. Worcestershire
½ tsp. ground mace	sauce
1 qt. milk	1 tsp. salt

To 1 quart canned tomatoes, add water and herbs; boil until tomatoes are done, about 45 minutes. Drop in a pinch of soda. May be made ahead until this point. Before serving, add 1 quart milk, worcestershire sauce, butter, salt, and pepper. Let it come to a simmer and serve immediately. Serve crushed crackers at table with soup.

—August, 1872

Eggs A La Bennett

½ finely chopped seeded green pepper	1½ C. milk
½ finely chopped medium onion	½ tsp. salt
	dash pepper
3 Tbs. butter	4 eggs
3 Tbs. Sauce and Gravy flour	4 slices country ham
½ C. cream	4 pieces toast

Make Creole sauce: Finely chop ½ seeded green pepper and ½ medium sized onion. Melt 3 Tbs. butter in saucepan. Cook pepper and onion slowly in butter until onion is transparent. Add 3 Tbs. flour and cook for three minutes without browning. Remove from fire and when cool add ½ cup cream, 1½ cups milk, ½ tsp. salt and dash pepper. Return to heat and cook until sauce thickens.

Poach 4 eggs, Heat 4 slices country ham. Toast 4 pieces toast. Put ham, egg, then sauce on each piece of toast and serve. Sprinkle with paprika.

Pears Poached in Wine

8 firm ripe pears   Vanilla—1 teaspoon,
3 cups sugar   lemon juice
3 cups dry white wine

Peel pears, cut bottoms off, if necessary, so pears will stand. Boil sugar and wine together, stirring until sugar dissolves. Add vanilla and lemon juice.

Add pears, simmer, basting continuously, until soft, about 15-20 minutes. Remove pears to serving dish, pour liquid over. Serve hot or cold, with whipped cream, sour cream, or make hot syrup of raspberry jam or other jellies (good on cold pears) or hot boiled custard.

Eating the Abbotsford Edition

AFTER THE Confederate War life was hard and everyone was poor. Uncle Julius Pringle made an arrangement with Mr. O'Hara, who sold old books, to buy a volume of "The Abbotsford Edition" of Sir Walter Scott when he wished to sell one. Uncle Julius found it hard to make up his mind to part with the Abbotsford Edition. I have forgotten who they thought they had to ask to dinner. The sacrifice had to be made. *Waverly* was sent to Mr. O'Hara. St. Julien Pringle, my cousin, was so excited, the next day he told me *Waverly* was a great success, so delicious and "would last several days." At that dinner, no one knew they were eating Sir Walter Scott's novel *Waverly*. Another time St. Julien came with a sad face—*Rob Roy* was tough, a failure. It was a long time before the whole of the Abbotsford Edition was sold. It was only sold when they were in great need of money. St. Julien and I were young and thought it funny to have dinners with such delightful names. We could not understand why as each novel was sold Uncle Julius was so sad. It seemed to make him sick, ill. He had a cheaper edition which we read whenever we wished—Abbotsford only to be looked at.

Medway

Mulberry

Menu

Light Lunch or Supper

Crab Soup

Broiled Oysters

Apple-Coconut Salad

Orange Ice with Lemon and Orange Peels Candied (p. 87)

Here is a delicious Fall meal for friends who enjoy good seafood.

Crab Soup

1 doz. crabs (1 lb. crabmeat)	Mace to taste
1 pt. milk	½ tsp. lemon juice
1 pt. cream	¼ C. cracker crumbs
½ stick butter	Sherry
Salt	Pepper

Simmer milk with mace and lemon juice in the top of a double boiler for a few minutes. Add crab, butter and cream and cook gently for 15 minutes. Add cracker crumbs and season with salt and pepper. Allow to stand for three minutes. Add 1 tbs. sauce flour if too watery. Add sherry before serving.

Broiled Oysters

1 doz. large oysters
Toast, buttered
Cream

Put large oysters on a wire toaster. Hold till heated through. Serve on toast moistened with warm cream.

Apple-Coconut Salad

½ coconut, grated (about ¾ C.)
2 apples, pared, cored and chopped
1 C. celery, chopped
2 level Tbs. onion (chopped)
1 Tbs. parsley, coarsely chopped
1 Chili pepper

Mix, cover with French dressing, and chill. Serve in lettuce shells or in scooped-out tomatoes.

Orange Ice

12 Oranges
4 Lemons
Sugar

Water
4 egg whites per quart

To the juice of 12 oranges and 4 lemons, add as much water as will reduce it to the desired strength (as you do for lemonade). Then, make it very sweet. To each quart of this add the whites of 4 eggs beaten to a strong froth. Freeze very quickly.

How Times Have Changed

THE OTHER afternoon a friend called. She told us she was so busy, that her daughter was going out this winter and she was giving her dinners and dances. There was no trouble in giving a dinner to her friends but to have any kind of entertainment for her daughter and *her* friends was a labor. It must be new and fashionable. They were severe critics and it was almost impossible to satisfy them. This made me think of the winter I went out. My first St. Cecelia ball was at the the South Carolina Hall. There were two long tables at the side of the room covered with fine damask, large dishes of biscuits, silver coffee pots. Biscuits and coffee were handed around. My father was president of the St. Cecelia at that time and Mr. Edward Milliken my father's friend who lived with us, was vice president. We all wore Tarlatan dresses, very pretty and always fresh. They were made at home by our mothers and sisters. We would meet at each others' houses and dance. We had nothing to eat, only water to drink. This went on for years. You never saw young people enjoy themselves more, so happy—they certainly had a good time. How times have changed!

The stopped sweeping to look at an automobile passing one of the first she had seen 1906

Sweeping

Menu

Light Lunch or Supper

Macaroni Soup

Tomatoes and Minced Meat Pie

Sivy Beans (small lima or butter beans)

Sally Lunn

Apple Float

Timing is of the utmost importance in preparing this meal. The tomato-macaroni soup base can be prepared the day before as can the tomato and minced pie. Actually, cook the pie and warm the soup, adding cream, before lunch and serve immediately.

The Sally Lunn is best started an hour before lunch and served warm. The apple float can be partially prepared (stewed apples) but should be put together minutes before serving.

Macaroni Soup

1 qt. boiling water (4 C.)	1 C. cream
1 handful macaroni	1 tsp. sugar
2 C. stewed tomatoes	dash pepper

To 1 quart water add 1 handful macaroni, (the elbow shaped or shells). Boil 1 hour. Add 2 C. strained, stewed tomatoes. Just before serving, add a cup of cream and a dash of pepper. Sugar helps cut the acidity.

Tomatoes and Minced Meat Pie

Sliced ripe tomatoes	Butter
Pound cold meat, cooked	Salt
Bread crumbs	Pepper

Put layers of sliced tomatoes, cold meat chopped fine and seasoned. Cover with bread crumbs seasoned and little bits of butter. Alternate tomatoes, chopped meat, and bread crumbs. Bake at 350° for 45 minutes. Serve immediately.

—Mrs. Ellen Porcher

Sivy Beans (Butter Beans)

1 qt. fresh sivy beans	Pepper
Salt	Butter

Wash with warm water, then cold. Cook in 2 qt. boiling, salted water for about 20 minutes. (Add ham bone while cooking.) Serve immediately with butter, and pepper as soon as they are tender. *Do not overcook.*

Sally Lunn

6 Tbs. good brown sugar	3 gills milk (1½ C.)
2 Tbs. melted butter	3 Tbs. baking powder
1 qt. flour (4 C.) plain	½ tsp. salt
3 eggs beaten separately	

Mix dry ingredients together. Then add slowly to the liquid. Mix all together folding in stiff egg whites and bake immediately. This quantity requires a very large pan, well greased, preferably a bundt pan. A ½ pound of currants is an improvement. Bake 40 minutes in a 350° oven.

Apple Float

1 qt. cooked apples	Whites of 4 eggs
6 Tbs. sugar	1 pt. cream
Nutmeg	

One quart of cooked apples mashed smooth. Sweeten with six tablespoonsful sugar, nutmeg. Add the apples a spoonful at a time to the well beaten whites of 4 eggs. Put 1 pint of thick cream in the dish and spoon apples and egg on top.

From the Ravenel Records

THE FAMILY of William Ravenel—William (a son of Daniel II of Wantoot plantation) born October 23, 1806, died November 10, 1888; married May 31, 1836 to Eliza Butler Pringle. The latter was born December 6, 1814, died August 6, 1888. She was a daughter of James Reid Pringle and his wife Elizabeth McPherson. The children by William and Eliza's marriage were as follows:

(1) Julia Pringle, born March 9, 1837, died June 4, 1863.
(2) Catherine Prioleau, born December 17, 1838, died March 6, 1933.
(3) James Reid Pringle, born June 1, 1840, died May 15, 1930.
(4) Elizabeth McPherson, born November 12, 1841, died April 9, 1928.
(5) Mary Pringle, born born November 16, 1843, died September 14, 1856.
(6) William, born December 20, 1845, died August 24, 1863.
(7) Edward, born January 4, 1848, died December 16, 1936. In December 1897 he married Wilhelmina Kruger.
* (8) ROSE PRINGLE, BORN FEBRUARY 28, 1850, DIED DECEMBER 3, 1943.
    THE AUTHOR OF *PIAZZA TALES, ROSE P. RAVENEL'S COOKBOOK.*
(9) Julius Pringle, born March 24, 1852, died May 7, 1853.

79

(10) Arthur Ravenel, born April 27, 1854, died April 30, 1855.

(11) Eliza Pringle, born October 18, 1856, died October 5, 1857.

Drawing of Tree at Farmfield by Lisa Smith

Menu

Breakfast or Brunch

Fresh Grapefruit

Drum Fish Roe

Omelette

Baked Eggs

Breakfast Biscuits

Orange Marmalade (p. 89)

This is a large party breakfast or brunch. The last three receipts can be prepared before hand.

The Drum fish roe is only available at certain times of the year. Any other roe may be more salty, and should be soaked overnight.

Fresh Grapefruit

Cut pink grapefruit in half, core, loosen, and serve.

Fish Roe

Drum roe   ½ lb. butter
3 pt. milk   1 lemon
2 Tbs. flour (all-purpose)

Wash large fresh Drum roe thoroughly in cold water and dry in a sieve. Have 3 pt. milk boiling. Tie roe in a towel (or cheesecloth) and boil in the milk for 20 or 30 minutes. Drain off milk. Reduce to half and thicken with flour and butter. Add one squeeze of lemon juice, salt and pepper to taste before serving. This makes the sauce to pour over the roe.

Omelette

1 or 2 eggs   3 Tbs. breadcrumbs
1 Tbs. butter   1 Tbs. parsley
Ground minced meat   Salt and pepper to taste

Beat the yolk and white of one or two eggs separately, then together. Add salt and drop into boiling butter for a few minutes. Turn it carefully but need not be turned. Take care that it is not too much done. A little parsley or meat minced may be added. It should rise and be quite light. The crumbs of a slice of bread can be added and rubbed up with the eggs. Serves two. Increase for proper amount for your guests.

Baked Eggs

6 or 8·eggs   2 Tbs. milk
2 Tbs. butter   3 Tbs. breadcrumbs
½ tsp. mustard   Some finely chopped
Dash pepper   cooked meat
Dash salt

Boil 6 or 8 eggs hard. Start them in cold water and when done throw into cold water. Peel and cut in halves. Take the

yolks and mash them well, adding butter, mustard, pepper, salt, milk and crumbs of bread. If it is fancied, add some finely chopped meat. Put most of this in a deep dish which must be buttered first and fill whites with the remainder. Set them into the mixture in the dish. Standing them up. Put the dish in the oven just long enough to heat and brown slightly.

Breakfast Biscuits

1 pt. (2 C.) all purpose flour	½ C. milk
4 tsp. baking powder	½ tsp. salt
2 Tbs. butter, heaping	

Mix dry ingredients first, then add liquid. Roll, not too thin, on floured board, and cut. Place on ungreased sheet without touching edges. Bake 10–12 minutes in 450° oven. (Keep dough soft, and use cold milk.)

Pickles, Candies, and Marmalade

Brandied Peaches

Tomato Pickle

Artichoke Pickle

Pickled Shrimp

Lemon and Orange Peels Candied

Groundnut Cakes

Creamed Chocolates

Orange Marmalade

Brandied Peaches

1 lb. fresh, firm peaches
1 C. sugar
brandy

Peel peaches and cut very thin. Put a layer of peaches, a layer of sugar, and let sit. When nearly covered in their own juice, place on fire and boil (about 5 minutes) until the syrup thickens. Put the peaches in jars and put as much brandy with the syrup as will cover them. (½ C. each) Pour it over and cork tightly. Keep for two weeks before serving. Serves 6–8.

—Mrs. Dawson

Tomato Pickle

1 peck green tomatoes
1 doz. onions
4 oz. mustard (ground)
1 oz. turmeric (ground)
1 oz. cloves (ground)
½ lb. white mustard seed
1 lb. brown sugar

1 oz. allspice
1 oz. ginger (ground)
1 oz. black pepper
  (ground)
8 bottles Spice Islands
  white wine vinegar

Slice the tomatoes and onions, sprinkle lightly with salt and let them stand two or three hours. Drain off the liquor and place in layers in the kettle, first of tomatoes and onions covered with spice until the kettle is full. Then cover with good strong vinegar and boil until tender. They are ready to use as soon as cold.

—Mrs. W. H. Mazyck 1889

Artichoke Pickle

4½ lbs. chopped artichoke
  (Jerusalem)
3½ lbs. of chopped cabbage
6 bell peppers chopped

1 qt. onions chopped
1 bunch of celery
  chopped
1 can pimiento chopped

Soak in 1 gal. of water and 2 C of salt for 2 hours
Sauce consists of—

2 qts. of vinegar, 3 lbs. of
    white sugar
1 C of flour
1 Tbs. of black pepper
3 Tbs. of dry mustard

2 Tbs. of celery seed
1 tsp. of powdered cloves
1 tsp. of powdered
    allspice

Boil, then pour over drained vegetables and let come to a boil.
Makes 16 pints.

—Miss Ethel Norvall

Pickled Shrimp

1 qt. peeled small shrimp
    (3 lb.)
1 Tbs. butter
1 dessert spoon allspice
    (1 tsp.)
1 dessert spoon ground
    pepper

1 dessert spoon salt
1 clove mace
1 pt. (2 C.) Spice Islands
    vinegar
1 pt. (2 C.) water in
    which shrimp were
    boiled

The shrimp must be washed carefully before boiling. Peel
the shrimp and squeeze juice out of the heads over them. Boil
vinegar and 2 C. of the water in which the shrimp have been
boiled with the allspice and mace added. Pour boiling hot
over the shrimp, butter, pepper, and salt.
    Drain before using. Place in bowl surrounded by ice and
have toothpicks nearby for serving.
    If to be bottled and kept, put rather more vinegar and less
water. Cork or seal tightly.

—Miss Rebecca Holmes

Lemon and Orange Peels Candied

6 oranges and/or 14 lemons
Salt

1 lb. sugar
1 qt. water

Cut the peels long ways and take out all the pulp. Put in
strong salt and water over night. Boil in plenty of water till

tender. Put in collander to drain. Place peels in cold water and bring to a boil. Drain. Repeat 3 times. This takes away some of the bitter taste.

Make a thin syrup of granulated sugar, one pound to one quart water. Put in the peels and boil over a slow fire until you see the syrup candy around the pan and peels are translucent. Lay out and grate fine sugar over them. Peels must be cooled completely or the sugar will not look "frosted". Lay coated peels on rack to dry. Store in container for future use. (When you boil lemons or oranges, do not cover the saucepan.)

—London Art of Cookery

Groundnut Cakes

1 lb. roasted, unsalted peanuts
1 lb. sugar (1½ C. is plenty)
1 tsp. vanilla (or rosewater)
3 egg whites (room temperature)

Chop peanuts in blender. Whip egg whites with pinch of salt until stiff. Add vanilla. Slowly add sugar, beating thoroughly. Add peanuts, mix well. Drop a teaspoonful on greased tins. Bake at 350° for 15–20 minutes, or until lightly brown. Batter will be thick. Makes approximately 5 dozen.

—Miss Milliken

Creamed Chocolates

1 egg white
2 Tbs. cold water
3½ C. 4-X confectioner's
sugar

1 tsp. vanilla or lemon
1 lb. sweet chocolate

Melt chocolate in double boiler.

Beat the egg and water together only till mixed; add the sugar until the ingredients form a *stiff* paste. Add flavoring and refrigerate the sugar mixture about an hour or until mixture can be formed into small balls. Dip in chocolate with a fork and then lay on waxed paper to harden. They may need to be dipped a second time. Refrigerate until ready to serve.

Orange Marmalade

3 lb. oranges
4½ lb. sugar
½ C. Orange juice

½ tsp. soda
2 C. water
1 bottle pectin

Choose good juice oranges, wash, and dry them. Lightly grate off the outer part of the oranges and cut them in half. Squeeze out the juice and pulp. Put the seeds aside. Boil the skins in sweetened water, (1 C.) until they are quite soft and have lost most of the bitter taste. Put a little soda in the water to keep the color the first time they are boiled.

When well boiled, add the pulp and 2 C. of the juice, and the remainder of the sugar. Add pectin and boil for 10 minutes.

Bottle in jars with secure screw-on tops.

INDEX

NOTES

NOTES

NOTES

NOTES

LaVergne, TN USA
18 January 2011
212895LV00004B/3/P

9 780872 496484